IT'S TIME TO EAT CHICKEN SLIDERS

It's Time to Eat CHICKEN SLIDERS

Walter the Educator

Silent King Books
A WhichHead Entertainment Imprint

Copyright © 2024 by Walter the Educator

All rights reserved. No part of this book may be reproduced in any manner whatsoever without written per- mission except in the case of brief quotations embodied in critical articles and reviews.

First Printing, 2024

Disclaimer

This book is a literary work; the story is not about specific persons, locations, situations, and/or circumstances unless mentioned in a historical context. Any resemblance to real persons, locations, situations, and/or circumstances is coincidental. This book is for entertainment and informational purposes only. The author and publisher offer this information without warranties expressed or implied. No matter the grounds, neither the author nor the publisher will be accountable for any losses, injuries, or other damages caused by the reader's use of this book. The use of this book acknowledges an understanding and acceptance of this disclaimer.

It's Time to Eat CHICKEN SLIDERS is a collectible early learning book by Walter the Educator suitable for all ages belonging to Walter the Educator's Time to Eat Book Series. Collect more books at WaltertheEducator.com

USE THE EXTRA SPACE TO TAKE NOTES AND DOCUMENT YOUR MEMORIES

CHICKEN SLIDERS

It's time to eat, come take a seat,

It's Time to Eat
Chicken Sliders

A special snack that's fun to eat!

Small and round, a tasty treat,

Chicken sliders can't be beat!

A soft, warm bun, so fluffy and light,

With chicken inside, cooked just right.

Grilled or crispy, take your pick,

These little sliders are gone so quick!

Add some cheese or a pickle slice,

A dash of ketchup, oh, so nice.

Maybe some lettuce, crisp and green,

Chicken sliders are a food dream!

Pick them up, they fit your hand,

They're small but mighty, oh so grand.

Take a bite and you will see,

How yummy chicken sliders can be!

It's Time to Eat
Chicken Sliders

They're juicy, tender, bursting with flavor,

Each little bite is one to savor.

With every chew, your smile will grow,

Chicken sliders steal the show!

Perfect for lunch or dinner, too,

A snack that's always made for you.

And if you're hungry for a lot,

Two or three will hit the spot!

With family or friends, they're fun to share,

Chicken sliders bring joy everywhere.

Line them up or stack them tall,

These tiny sandwiches please us all!

Dip them in sauce, if that's your thing

Barbecue or ranch? Let the flavor sing!

They're messy, sure, but that's okay,

It's Time to Eat
Chicken Sliders

Chicken sliders brighten your day.

And when you're full, you'll say with glee,

"Chicken sliders were perfect for me!"

So next time hunger gives a call,

Chicken sliders are best of all!

So grab a slider, take a bite,

They'll fill your tummy and feel so right.

Little and yummy, made with care,

It's Time to Eat Chicken Sliders

Chicken sliders are beyond compare!

ABOUT THE CREATOR

Walter the Educator is one of the pseudonyms for Walter Anderson. Formally educated in Chemistry, Business, and Education, he is an educator, an author, a diverse entrepreneur, and he is the son of a disabled war veteran. "Walter the Educator" shares his time between educating and creating. He holds interests and owns several creative projects that entertain, enlighten, enhance, and educate, hoping to inspire and motivate you. Follow, find new works, and stay up to date with Walter the Educator™

at WaltertheEducator.com

www.ingramcontent.com/pod-product-compliance
Lightning Source LLC
LaVergne TN
LVHW052011060526
838201LV00059B/3966